HER

Way with Words

Reviews for Her Way with Words

"They say I got this way with words... and every time I blush and say 'nah I'm just telling my story...'
Unapologetically raw. Brianna's debut chapbook Her Way with Words brings the reader into her world. A page turner that will make you want to read it, and then read it again."

— Bella Soleil , author of Side Effects of Remembering the Little Things

"What an intriguing garden of a book, one that invites you to go deep into its soil. There is the best of performance poetry put on the page here, complete with the modern aesthetics of her experience. But there is also the influential seeds of Jayne Cortez's black english bending wordplay, and the organic open field experiments of June Jordan and Dolores Kendrick. In the big packages of these poems is a genuine talent that Portland should protect at all cost"

— Robert Lashley, author of Up South and The Homeboy Songs

"Briana Renae writes poems that seek witness while holding tribute to Black family, community, culture, and magic. These poems are an insistent voice, uncovering the overlooked: those suffering from chronic illness, stolen neighborhoods, and love that upends everything you think you know."

— Amber Flame, author of Ordinary Cruelty

HER

Way with Words

———

BRIANNA RENAE

Acknowledgements

I would like to acknowledge the people and organizations that have helped me reach this moment.

I would like to start off by thanking Portland Poetry Slam and Slamlandia for pushing me to challenge myself as a poet and competitor.

I would like to thank Literary Arts for connecting me with opportunities for an aspiring writer to network.

Thank you to my editor Sam Preminger for all of your hard work and talent.

Thank you to Vivian Lihonde for creating the book cover of my DREAMS.

Most importantly I would like to thank my family for teaching me unconditional love. Thank you to my mother for teaching me the power of linguistics. Thank you to my father for teaching me to choose happiness. Thank you to my siblings Khayman, Kayla, and Flenny, for the memories and inspiration. This would not have been possible without the unique qualities every single one of you brought to my life. I love y'all so much.

Lastly, I obviously have to thank Beyoncé for inspiring this brown girl to push boundaries ever since I was eight years old.

This book is dedicated to my ancestors.

I was robbed of their stories,
but their sacrifices
allow me to tell mine.

Table of Contents

Her Way with Words

Her Way with Words

They say I got this way with words...
and every time I blush and say
"Nah, I'm just telling my story."
See I'm bashful,
quiet,
the wallflower type.
Always sittin' back
observin'
comparing what I see
to what I read in my psychology textbooks.
I like to make things make sense more than I like to talk,
but when I do speak

they say I got this way with words...
warm,
soft,
but powerful.
The capability to take a tongue dip-dyed in trauma
and use it to paint a map of all the places I've ever been,
to create a reminder that no matter where I go
I am still *Her*.
No matter how hard I try leave parts of Her
at rock bottom
I am constantly reminded that I need all of Her
to get back to the top.

Sometimes I forget,
but this map reminds me
I love Her.
I carry Her highs and lows in my eyes,
so you may catch me spacing out,
you may catch me making myself small
so I can make room for the burdens I picked up on the way,
but I always unpack.

Organize.
Destroy.
Rebuild.
Grow.
Evolve.
All once I get back home.
They tell me this is called poetry,

I say *this is just me.*
This is what happens when you give an introvert a microphone,
when you tell a person covered in camouflage
they are on fire
and you can still see them.
See at times I feel invisible,
but I make myself known when the smoke gets too thick,
when I need to tell the story of how I survived the flame,
of how I became the flame.
I do it for Her,

she who can sometimes make life with her womb,
but can always change lives with her words.
For Her
whose walk will break necks,
whose passion will break barriers,
both without her trying.
To Her
sis is just existing,
sis is just surviving,
sis is evolving into everything she needs to be,
sis is learning she is already all of that.
Blessed be those that can learn from the way she lives,
breathes,
the way she perceives life.

I have inherited the world
a million times around,
it resides inside me
so if I seem lost,
oblivious,
disconnected from reality,
it is because I am exploring the universe inside of me.

2

I am listening.
I am learning.
I call this meditation.
This is how I make it make sense.
This is how I keep Her alive

so when I do speak,
I will close my eyes
and pour out lessons from those who no longer can
onto anyone willing to transform
because to be woman
and alive
with a voice
is a privilege I do not always feel worthy of,
so I will always dedicate it
to show the world who I am,
because I am Her
and this is
Her Way with Words.

BRIANNA RENAE

I.

BRIANNA RENAE

My First Whole Foods

i.

I remember discovering Whole Foods at the simple age of 10
– they built it across the street from my father's and
grandfather's barbershop.

ii.

In the summer my brother and I would ride my bike
down 15th street until we reached the bottom,
ready to clock in at our first job.
Sweeping floors.
$20 a day, or $15 if we complained too much...
it was usually $15.

My brother and I looked forward to those $15 dollars,
spending it all across the street. See, back then
Whole Foods was like our own shopping mall.
My brother and I would check every day
to see if the pepperoni pizza was two for $5
(the biggest slices we had ever seen!).
We'd rush to the frozen food section
picking out the most delicious (and only)
gluten-free mac n' cheese we'd ever tasted.
I'd stroll down the locally produced aisle,
try on the tester bottle of Pacifica's Hawaiian Ruby Guava
perfume – a scent of my childhood.
I'd stare at the overpriced pastries.
I'd joke with my brother
"One day, I'm going to have enough money to buy all of them."

iii.
For years this Whole Foods was home
away from home, but a day came when I realized
I was no longer a cute little girl coming in for cheap pizzas.
Perhaps I never was.
Perhaps I was too blinded by my daily new discoveries
to realize that I was the one being discovered...
I'm not sure if it was passive racism
or if they were just amazed to know Black people still live here.

One day I went with my father to buy a salad.
We saw there were samples by the line
        where they always were,
vegan and organic
        like they'd always been,
and as my father reached to grab one
        like he always did,
a white man grabbed my father by the wrist,
told him "wait your turn."
My father is vegan
My father loves organic food
My father had been on this block
longer than that white man had been alive.

My father is also a six-foot-tall Black man.

One 911 call from becoming a hashtag, my father
held back his rage. That day
I learned the dangers of white stares.

iv.

Years later, the owner of my family's barbershop
decides to lease the building to a white franchise.
My grandfather is robbed of his three other properties by
predatory lenders.
Losing things has become a norm for my family and
I can't help but to wonder

When did I become a tourist in my own hood?
Was this ever a hood?
Was this ever mine?

v.

Today when I drive by dad's old shop
I look inside just to find a white woman
touching up a white man's
"dreadlocks."
This moment is the epitome of what it means to be
a Black Portlander:
my gut tells me to throw a trash can through the window
and flip their colonizing asses the bird.
Instead, I think of a woman.

My dad did this woman's hair since before I was born.
Growing up, she'd give me advice about men
and my dad would roll his eyes all annoyed,
but I just laughed in confusion. She was sitting right there
where that white man is. I wonder
Where is she now?
Where are any of us now?
Then I look at the Whole Foods across the street.

vi.

Since my first time in Whole Foods I've seen
at least three more pop up in my city. In this city,
I feel less and less comfortable walking
inside. Maybe I'm just paranoid.
Maybe they don't have anything against me.
This is progressive Portland, right?
And the Black Lives Matter sign should chill my anxiety,
but I don't think gluten-free mac n' cheese can satiate
the hole in my soul that was once filled by a Black Portland,
now replaced by Whole Foods and another
Whole Foods that attracts middle class white people
with their fear of the Black people who managed to stay...

But it's one of the things you get used to, you know?

Like U-Haul's in front of minority houses.
Like "closed for business" signs on your favorite restaurants.
Like white folks asking
"How are you from here if you've never been to
[name of a place Black people would never go]?"
Like seeing people bike down Killingsworth street butt naked
for fun
and knowing they would be afraid to step foot on this block
ten years ago
if they knew how many killings it's seen.
Like watching mayors rebuilding schools in North Portland
even though the Black kids that needed it
are no longer here to reap the benefits.
Like apartment hunting for fun,
like a joke. Telling myself
           "I'm going to afford to live here, one day."

Sick Kids

I was fourteen years old when I was diagnosed with
Crohn's Disease.
Pain was my first love.
Broken was my identity.
I considered it a great day if I was able to spill out the words
"I'm fine"
without crying
and people actually believed me,
but in reality
every day I wished to time travel so far back
and warn my parents
"Do not conceive me the way you believe, old-fashionedly,
and *maybe*
put me in a test tube and dissect away my flaws
so I can function well enough
You know, the way that the rest do?"

So today I dedicate this poem to us *sick kids*.
The ones society,
oh so quietly,
pushed to the back burner for so long
they forgot that we exist, forgot we learn to excel,
refuse to grant us our wings because we have been
dragged through hell.

For all of us molding against waiting room walls,
anxiously trying to classify our pain from a 1 to a 10,
but getting stuck every time because we could have sworn
last time was a 10,
but now we feel like 10 times worse than then
so we guess and say something like 7 and pray we'll never
endure an 8 again.

This poem is for all of us that used to speak so clearly
with diction,
for all of us that used to stand so tall, fist up high,
like Lady Liberty,
but are now hunched over, stuttering, holding the blade
that reality stabbed us with yesterday
and twisted
and twisted
until we bled out every able-bodied fantasy.

This poem
is for the sick kids. This poem is for me, for my
crimson hands dripping and shaking,
when I look in the mirror and don't
recognize what I see.

I want to disown my reflection and run away,
but I am snatched back by clichés
I hear every damn day:
BRIANNA!
Why do you deserve an A? You weren't even in class today!

But teacher can't you see?
I've been busy
crawling up that Mt. Everest of makeup homework
you've already assigned to me.
Just because you don't notice the bruises on my knees
does not mean I stopped climbing.
Teacher, *please,*
I NEED you to stop mistaking our stories for an excuse.
I want you to know I come to you inspired
and as my anemic fingers turn the pages
to my African American History homework,
I become lit on *fire*

by the concept that three hundred years ago my own people
were slaves
and here I am today, a slave to my own body
and a broken system,
but I am NO victim.

It is literally in my DNA to break free
from your half-ass sympathetic expectations of me.

This poem
will never be a poem begging for sympathy,
this is using my story as request for respect for me
and my chronically ill patience
that often runs empty.

This poem is for the practice
of waking up every day and silently silencing
all the tragic statistics,
not perfect,
but *sweet* and *unique* like buttermilk biscuits.

This poem is for *us*
with the courage to fight
without fear of which climb will be our last,
for if we fall today
we will be remembered tomorrow.

So if you have the privilege to see us today,
know we are all so much more than sick kids.

Promise you will never forget that
when you tell our story
tomorrow.

-

Questions From Grown Ups

Babygirl,
why you sway your hips
if not an invitation to dance?
Why you lubricate your lips
if you don't wanna kiss?
And why you put on that tank top?
Don't you know bare shoulders
feed the curiosity of *grown men?*
Don't you know what happens to young girls
with *a body like yours?*
Don't you know in *your* garden there are no
forbidden fruits?

Babygirl,
why you so upset?
Don't you know rappers write songs
about girls like you?
Don't you know you get your sexy from your mama,
and your silence from her too?
Don't you know you can't act fast
and expect a man with needs to take it slow?
Don't you know you can't jump rope like that no more?
Don't you know girls that blossom too fast
always get picked first
and it only takes adultification to justify this thirst?

Babygirl,
all that I am saying
is *with a body like that* can you blame me,
for not treating you
like a baby?

BRIANNA RENAE

African-American

We considered it an upgrade
from when we were tired of being called colored
or simplified down to Black,
but I personally think hyphenating
a continent to a country - when neither really claim you
is honestly quite sad.
But still I claim that I'm Black and I'm proud
and sometimes I can be loud!
Just, you know,
not in front of large white crowds.

Being Black in America is sort of like being
a child lost in the grocery store.

Everyone wants to help get me back to my parent
until I tell them I can't remember her name,

until the instant I'm adult enough to get shoved
outside to the street, desperately
taking in labels they spare for me like loose change—

Nigga. Queen. Pretty for a Black girl.

Then comes my favorite question:
"I don't see color, why should you?"
But pardon me for believing when you claim you
"don't see color"
you're really implying you don't see me
'cause when I needed help color was all you could see,
'cause I've been coming to this grocery store 24 years,
but every day I walk in and out stared at
like an animal escaped from the zoo.
But not in a *racist* way.

In a "hey you're different—
can't I touch?

take pics?
embrace it?" way.
An *appropriate* it way.

But my culture has always been up for grabs.
African-American
so many feel entitled to half.

Nothing in this damn store is *mine*—
The way I do my hair.
The way I rock my rhymes.
Down to the way I am oppressed.

I yell "Black Lives Matter," but they
just convince me that there is plenty of oppression in the sea,
not realizing this makes me drift further
and further from my identity,
'cause not knowing who you are
is to not know what it means to matter.
And if I had a dollar for every time I was asked
"So where you really from?"
by someone that looks uncomfortably like me,
and I hesitated for far too long...

Well let's just say I'd have enough money
for a premium membership to *ancestry.com,*
enough money to feel closer to mama Africa, but
I'm not even sure if she remembers me.
MAMA
Do you hear me call out your name from aisle 13?
Mama look I'm free, but I still feel unseen.
Mama... do you like the portrait I got of you on my back?
Most of the time I can't see it,
but I'm comforted by the idea that it's there.
Mama it's been over 400 years since I've seen you,
but I know you're in here
and maybe the way that I talk, combined with my last name
and the weave in my hair makes me not African enough.
But I do not care.
And maybe my brown skin

and vocalized opinions about racism in this country
make me not American enough.
But I'm here to stay.
And whether it was my choice or not,
this is where I belong.
So yes
I wear this African American confusion like a crown.
Yes sometimes it's heavy and it weighs me down,
but it's mine!
And I promise from now on every Whole Foods,
New Seasons,
and Trader Joe's I strut into
will see my shine!

BRIANNA RENAE

Sitcom Dad

They're trying to make us believe that Black men
do not take care of their children.
They tried to break apart our families with
mass incarceration,
welfare,
and propaganda like *Love and Hip Hop.*

They are trying to erase the efforts of the Black father figures
that fertilized the soil of the family tree
we all grow from.
They are trying to teach us that the nurture
embedded in your dna
has been mutated into toxic masculinity.

So this poem is a dedication
to the *real Black fathers,*
the ones who grew up without fathers,
the ones who swore to be nothing like their fathers

or everything like their fathers,
the ones that break generational curses,
the new Black fathers
that are doubting if they have the tools,
the broke Black fathers
that can make a dollar stretch a weekend,
the tv Black fathers
who fill the void of all the ones that are not with us.

This poem is a dedication to *my father.*
As I grew up watching all the classics,
I did not realize I could find all the sitcom dads in one man,
my provider.

Daddy you are,
hilarious like Uncle Bernie,
financially reserved like Julius,
embarrassing like Andre Jonson,
hip like Flex Washington,
stubborn like Micheal Kyle,
wise like Uncle Phil,
fashionably loud like Pops,
old school like George Jefferson,
sensitive like Randall Pearson,
an entrepreneur like Oscar Proud,
comforting like Victor Baxter,
and *supportive* like Mr. Henderson,

and I find this to be no coincidence.

Even though the world painted you
beast,
super predator,
nigger,

you still became an absorbent for all the
goodness you've experienced,
for what it really means to be
Black,
father,
and *here.*

You are here when the world said you couldn't be.
You are at every tea party,
dance recital,
basketball game,
emergency room visit,
crosswalk intersection,
poetry competition.

You are always here
and not just for your biological children.
You bring out what it means to be a positive

Black male role model
to the young Black children around you.

They look forward to playing rocket with you,
to showing you they can free throw just like Kobe,
to learning how to tie a tie from you,
to being silly with you
when the media doesn't show them how to.
They may not tell you,
but just like those *sitcom dads,*
there are so many children thinking
"I want to grow up and be a good dad, just like you."
This is how the positive cycle continues,
this is how barriers formed against you
are shattered.

So this is dedication to say
Black fathers, *we see you*
and we are so thankful,
even if mom always get the better gifts
and we typically call her first.
Black fathers,
nothing in this world could ever
replace your worth.

BRIANNA RENAE

Smile, Babygirl

Everyone says they love my smile.
My dad says it's my greatest attribute,
ever since I was a little girl in the emergency room
he'd take my hand and say
"Keep smiling baby girl. You'll bounce back soon."

Age 14

50 pounds lighter than 13.
Desperate for answers.
My doctor finally walks in
"Brianna you have something called Crohn's disease.
There is no cure."
Confused,
frightened,
yet somewhat relieved,
I look at my dad, smile, and say *okay*
even though we both knew
I was not going to bounce back soon.

Age 15

I wake up every day to the sound of my parents
getting my siblings ready for school.
I had hopes that their morning routine and plans for the day
were louder than my body begging to get ready too.
I hate being alone,
but I wish mornings would go by faster.
Every morning
I place a blanket over my malnourished body.
Every morning
I hide my medicine bin under the couch.
I do not want my siblings to see this

prescription crossword puzzle
that my body now depends on.
I do not want my mom to see the bags under my eyes.
I stayed up all night watching Nick at Nite,
wishing the Fresh Prince could make me laugh
the way it used to,
wishing I could sleep
the way I used to,
wishing I could do literally anything
the way I used to,
but instead I smile,
wish them a great day.
I remind them their big sis will be okay.

Age 16

Every time someone calls my phone,
I wait until the last ring to answer.
I need this time to find the words
"I'm going to be alright"
because they couldn't feel any further.
My grandma calls today,
tells me she's coming by, asks if I could grab
church pants from my brother's room,
but if I can't, "it's okay!"
I wish I could tell her that the arthritis
from my hands and feet
has prevented me from going upstairs for weeks
and there is nothing okay about it,
but okay is all I want to be.
So I smile through the phone and tell her "yes"
and prepare for my journey up the stairs.
I crawl and cry for ten minutes every three steps.
Elbows, knees, cry, repeat.
Elbows, knees, cry, repeat.
I have to make it up these stairs
and when they are finally conquered
my grandma calls and says she actually can't make it,
but she loves me.
I say "it's okay, grandma"
and I hang up the phone

and I break down for hours until my parents come home.
I wipe my tears before they come to check on me,
as they always do,
but something about my smile
must have been shakier than usual
because my mom is staring right through the wall I put up.
I've never said it out loud,
but through gazing blankly at the tv
I'm begging her to *stop looking at me.*
I know it only takes 17 muscles to smile,
but those are losing the battle
against the 40 it takes to frown.
Mama, please don't knock this wall down.
I wish I could beg my mom to lay in this bed
and wrap her arms around
without touching me.
The warmth of her loving heart
should never feel the coldness of this loveless body,
a body of love would never do this to me.
Mama, please stop looking.
Mama, please don't take this smile away from me!
It is the only thing I'm still good at.
I take a deep breath,
prepare to surrender my strength
when dad intercepts,
"Keep smiling baby girl.
We know you will bounce back soon."
And smiling is what I do
because I'm supposed to.

Age 24

People still say they love my smile.
Sometimes my facial expression turns a bit odd.
I guess it's because I'm shocked that
this smile is still doing its job.

Meeting Your Long-Distance Lover for the First Time Feels Like

The fastest six hour flight I've ever been on.
It took 12 sessions of convincing my parents
he wasn't a serial killer,
18 lectures from friends about how I'm too naïve,
1 maxed out credit card,
and a 3 hour layover,
but somehow it seems like I got here in the blink of an eye.

I wasn't sure how to prepare for this moment,

so I spent most of my flight listening to meditations
hoping I wouldn't have a panic attack when we met.
It didn't work,
I'm still freakin' out as soon as I touch down in his city
—Miami, Florida—
(I would pick the boy that lives as far across the country as possible,
3,925 miles away,
but I've never felt closer to anyone).

I'm okay with my heart strings pulling me across the country

as long as the boy I love and the tropical paradise
are waiting for me on the other side.
When I land, I turn my phone off airplane mode,
get a text:
"I'm here at the airport, let me know when you land babe"
My heart drops.
I take my carry-on bag and run to the bathroom,
reapply edge control to my baby hairs,
apply my favorite beauty supply store lips gloss,
pop on some oversized hoop earrings

Giving this airport basicness a little razzle dazzle.
Deodorant? Check.
Boobs? Check.
Goofy ass smile from ear to ear? Check.

BREATHE!

I tell myself to calm down,
don't make it dramatic like the YouTube videos.
Stay calm, cool, and collected
which works
until I catch the first glimpse of him
pulling up to me in his car
(it's hot as hell by the way)
and this first-time eye contact
along with Florida humidity has me sweating out
EVERYTHING.

He rushes out of the car.
He trips,
breaking the ice I swore I was
going to melt from breathing so hard.

I laugh.
He laughs,
catches his feet and runs over to me.
He says *hello.*

My heart beats faster than Nick Cannon's solo in Drumline.
I am looking at the man I've spent the last four months
loving through a screen, but he's here in 3D
and he's staring at me,
talking to me
with a real ass voice,
hugs me with his real ass arms,
and he smells really...
good.
I've wondered what he's smelled like for four months
and he has exceeded all expectations.
I am drowning in this overwhelmingly beautiful reality.
        Say something.

Say something.
But I am speechless,
so instead I just kiss him

and we blush like it was the first kiss either of us ever had.

He puts my bags in the backseat,
opens my door,
we buckle up.
He puts his hand on my thigh,
smiles,
asks
"You ready babe?"
and it feels like a movie.
I kiss his hand,
"Let's go get em."
And we drive off into what feels like
happily ever after.

This feels like the beginning
of the greatest story I will ever tell.

BRIANNA RENAE

II.

BRIANNA RENAE

Getting Dumped by Someone You Never Dated

Dang Bri, *AGAIN!?*
When will you learn?
Let me guess, *this one was different?*
You thought things were going to change?
Why do you expect different results
when your approach stays the same?
It's like a guy will tell you
"I'm hurting.
I never loved a woman.
I am depressed.
I don't know how to accept love.
I will probably hurt you."
And all you hear is
PERFECT.
And what do you do?
Go to the back of your closet,
grab your purple cape
and turn into Captain Save-A-Negro
because you think you can fix everyone
even though
you know you want a commitment,
you know you want roses on your birthday.
Yet you ask "how high?"
when the boy that always forgets your b-day
asks you to jump.
And why?
Why?
It's not because you do not know your worth,
you just bargain a little more
when they have sad puppy dog eyes.
It's not because you need a man,
it's because you think their need to finally feel love

the right way,
trumps your need to be properly valued for the first time.
You think if you do all the right things
they will undoubtedly see how great love is
and it will all be worth it
and **CONGRATULATIONS**
look what that gets you!
A tall, brown skin boy
that you can't keep,
you just cry over!
Unfortunately,
your prize doesn't include validation for your tears,
but you do get a shit load of guilt for getting your hopes up.
You will stalk his social media to find signs that he's hurting,
thinking maybe there's a chance he didn't mean it
when he said "we can't do this anymore."
You squeezed onto *"this"* so tightly, for so long
that now you are left only with swelling in your fingers
bowling-ball sized self-pity in your gut
and *"how did I get here?"*
written across your forehead.
You hoped this wouldn't happen,
but you fell for another boy
who will never feel the same way about you
and as shitty as it feels,
you will never regret it
because that's who you are—
unconditional love pours out of every wound
this hard life gave you.
Every time a boy hurts you
you commit to loving the next one ten times harder.
You never give up
and when a boy
tells you
"I am not worthy of your love"
instead of looking the other way
you say "I'll show you that you are"
and while some will never be ready to hear that,
they will never forget that
you show love.
You are love.

Blessed be anyone, deserving or not,
that comes in contact with your love,
but you have to admit
being dumped by someone you never dated feels shitty
and that matters.
The empty vase on your coffee table matters.
The leaking hole in your heart matters.
Once you soak up the love
that so desperately pours out of you
you will realize
it is way too pure
to ever be bargained for.

Preference vs Prejudice

My entire life I've had this confusion
when it came to the difference between
preference and prejudice.

I noticed that the world seems to be lost, too.

So I've decided to separate a few general phrases
to see if we could recognize the difference:

Preference
I prefer to work out at 24 Hour Fitness.

> *Prejudice*
> *LA Fitness ain't shit.*

Preference
I prefer bacon and bbq sauce on my cheeseburger.

> *Prejudice*
> *If you put mustard on my burger I will kill you.*

Preference
I prefer when my hair is straight, that's when it looks best.

> *Prejudice*
> *Nappy hair just looks so unprofessional.*

Preference
I prefer light-skinned women.

> *Prejudice*
> *I will date Asian, white, Latina, Hawaiian—*
> *anything, but Black women.*

It's not my fault they aren't my preference.

Preference
I prefer pretty women.

> Prejudice
> Because you don't fit my box of what I believe a
> woman should look like, smell like, weigh like,
> dress like, I have the right to remind you that
> you will never be enough for me cause that's my
> preference.

> Prejudice-
I mean, Preference
I prefer to not be called out on my preferences.

> Prejudice
> I'm so sick of you insecure bitches telling me what I
> can and can't like.
> I'm so sick of people not letting me uphold
> European beauty standards.
> How dare you call me out on my preferences?

As you can see there is a thin line between
preference and prejudice, especially when they both root
back to the same racist tongue.

Preference is the butter knife,
> Prejudice is the butcher knife,
but both can kill if you apply enough pressure...
pressure to look like what America wants you to look like
> so you can be happy,
> have a good job,
> so you can find love,
> so you can find what so many die trying to.

Get closer to white, or *die trying to.*

Colorism is a nationwide problem
so much bigger
than you preferring Karrueche over Lupita.

Yes, you have the right to like what you like,
but that is not what this conversation is about.

This conversation is about Black children
getting sent home from school,
because their educators prefer their Black students
not wear their hair
the way it grows out of their head.

This conversation is about generations of children
that consistently chose the white doll as
safer,
prettier,
and more successful
than the Black doll.

And we wonder why we grow up and say things like
      "I'm pretty for a Black girl, right?"
Because we know Black is not the world's preference
so we are taught that the most we can be
is an exception.

And to be clear
this is not an insecure girl problem,
this is global anti-blackness, disguised as preference
that we are all guilty of perpetuating
no matter how many documentaries,
no matter how many poems,
because we still refuse to call it what it is...

This is a problem.
A problem I alone can not fix,
but I damn sure will talk about it.

BRIANNA RENAE

Summer Nights at the Club Feel Like...

The "More Life" Drake was always talking about,
Feels like the epitome of when Jacquees said
"21 with no kids."
I probably only have $2 in my bank account,
but I'ma party like my pockets are bottomless.
My girls come through and we lookin like a
2019 Destiny's Child.
Okay maybe not that good,
but pretty damn close.
We got on our skintight Fashion Nova jeans,
our snakeskin body suits
with the cleavage OUT,
thigh high boots that reach our pelvis,
Fenty Gloss Bomb on our lips,
highlight bright enough to blind someone,
45 seconds of selfie videos
because tonight we are in our *bag!*
Tonight there is
no stressin',
no arguin' with our boos.
All we gotta worry about is getting to the club before 11,
but let's be real,
we never get to the club before 11.
Perfection take times
and so does back to back shots of dark liquor
because light will have us ready to fight.
We pull up in Chinatown like the pretty young thangs
legends sing about,
feeling like we wish somebody would try to kill our vibe.
Tonight is about *us.*
Tonight is history in the making.
When my future kids ask me what I used to be like

I'm not going to tell them,
but I'll think of this night.
The *bumpin' and grindin'*,
pretty girl rockin',
twerkin' to whatever Cardi B song is poppin',
drinking back to back AMF's
even though I told myself last time
I was done with the AMF's.
Soaking up the free drinks we got
from the section we were invited to
because in a room full of shy Portland dudes
you want the pretty
turnt up,
trippin over their own two feet,
lit girls at your table,
but please believe when they play
"Cash Money Records taking over for the '99 and the 2000"
me and my girls will dip like ranch
and make our way to the dance floor
cause *damn we look good*
and we will for sure *back dat ass up*
because if we are going to be ratchet for a night
we might as well make it look *sexy,*
we might as well have fun,
might as well dance like no one is watching
even though *everyone* is always watching
so we will LAUGH,
let loose
and not give a damn what you think
because there is so much pressure
to not uphold ghetto Black girl stereotypes
Monday through Friday,
but Saturdays are for *US.*
On Saturday we live like Sunday isn't going to happen,
but when Sunday does happen,
and reality sets back in
we gotta wake up extra early and delete the Snapchat story,
pretend like I don't know that girl screaming
"AYEEE FUCK IT UP BITCHHH"
at the top of her lungs.
She's gone now

So when you see my posting motivational quotes
Sunday morning
like I wasn't throwin' it back all night before,
mind ya business.

I Believe You

In a world that treats victims as defendants,
as liars until proven attacked,
I'd like to take the time to say, no matter the circumstances,
I believe you.
Even if you were blacked out drunk and barely remember.
Even if your rapist is beloved by the community.
Even if they seemed harmless in the beginning.
Even if you didn't scream.
Even if you said no, but were coerced into giving consent.
I believe you.

Even if your abuser is a woman.
Even if your abuser is family.
Even if your abuser was your partner.
Even if you still love them.
Even if you don't really remember.
Even if you don't want to remember.
Even if it doesn't feel real anymore.
Even if you continued to be with them.
I believe you.

Even if you are a sex worker.
Even if you love to show off your body.
Even if you convinced yourself you gave them the wrong idea
—you know you did not, *and I believe you.*
Even when society draws a picture of the perfect victim
and it looks nothing like you.
Even if you have been "dramatic" your entire life.
Even if it took you 15 years to talk about it.
Even if you've never said the words out loud.
Even if you have not one single proof.

I still believe you
Because for every one person that falsely accuses

there are thousands of victims silenced by
fear that everyone will see them as that *one.*

Because out of 100 rape cases,
only 3 rapists are likely to see the inside of a jail cell
and with the way rape culture is set up
I bet even fewer are aware they are rapists.

Because 94% of survivors experience some sort of PTSD
and many times it's not just from their attackers,
but from the ones who listened to their story
and called them a *slut,*
whore,
attention-seeking liar
as if this attention was ever something anyone would seek.

I simply believe you
because the reality is
all of the above means absolutely nothing,
sexual assault is not always black and white
and healing is almost never linear.
The only thing that matters is that you are a **survivor.**

I do not need to know another goddamn thing.
You are still here.
Your body is still yours.
Your pain matters.
You matter.
They are a piece of shit,
but this poem is not about them.
This poem is for you.
I believe you
and I'm so sorry that happened to you.

Even though I can not take the pain away
or promise you justice
I can guarantee that through your *screams,*
cries,
and even *silence,*
I promise to ALWAYS stand by you.

Black Girl Magic?

To the white woman that called #BlackGirlMagic
"Reverse Racism"
I just wanna say...

I get it.

Growing up in Portland — well, anywhere really —
you have the privilege of everything being accessible to you.
I can imagine how me claiming something as
exclusively mine
could feel like your version of racial oppression...
for the first time,
but lucky for you
I have free front row seats to a few tricks
I can manifest at the snap of my Black wrist:
BOOM *like magic*
watch how fast I float like a butterfly
when you try to touch my new hairdo in the workplace,
watch how even faster I get stung like a bee by my boss
for having the audacity to come in
looking so unkempt in the first place,
but *Presto*: two seconds into my timeline and you'd discover
Kim K's "New Trendy Urban Braids".

The same braids I've been rockin' since I was eight.

The same braids I almost lost my job for today.

My magic is obtaining the world's most desirable culture
and the world's most unprotected demographic
at the same damn time.
It is to walk into a Portland business
and simultaneously be the most stared at
and most ignored person there.
It is to be stereotyped as the LOUDEST race,

then get told no one hears me when I have something to say.

Still not a believer?
Watch how fast I make America smile
when I pull out my debit card then
BOOM *like magic*
I make mouths drop when I pull out the "race card"
as if the quality of my existence
could be pulled out of my back pocket like a library card
and despite the cards I've been dealt,
I turn my trauma into performance constantly
because my skin alone is not enough to qualify me as the
unthreatening type of Black girl,
so maybe some poems will?

This still may be abstract for you,
but you must recognize I, a Black woman,
can take three hundred years of repressed Black hate,
flip it into a three-minute poem,
perform it for an audience that maybe
three other Black people are in,
score a ten

and you're going to look me in the eyes

and tell me that's not magic?

....don't get me wrong.

      If you did, you'd be right.

There is nothing magical about the way this country expects
Black women to fight.
Democrats always say they want
Michelle to save this country,
I say, she didn't make the mess so
she should not have to bear the burden of that job.
I laid down to write a "*Black Girl Magic*" poem
and I found myself explaining my existence
to another white woman
in hopes that she doesn't get offended
      that she's **not** welcome in it,
      but that's **not** my job

and this is **not** magic.
This is called ***surviving.***

Everyone wants to be a part of Black culture
where it's thriving,
but not where our people are dying.

And to all the Black women
that hold this weight on our backs,
the Black women the world calls magic
for the million ways *y'all* twist and bend our backs,
yet we never snap—
        WE ARE DONE WITH THAT.
This show is no longer for y'all.
This is for us,
by us,
and your opinion of how we do us does not matter.
And if you *still* have a problem,
please refer to my final trick
as I bend over just enough
for you to plant a kiss
on my magical Black ass.

Being a Black Woman is Lit

Being a Black woman is lit.
In translation, *everything about us is fire.*
From our sun-kissed melanin
once captivated by western hate
that we learned to embrace so graciously
to the rhythm in our stomp,
from the dance floor to the protests,
from the trendiness of our precisely parted cornrows
to the nurture bound to our charisma.
To be Black and woman is to reside on an intersection that
everyone tries to gentrify,
but we are worth way more than offers from low bidders
that couldn't couldn't survive a week without us.
        We run this block.
From the way we started BlackLivesMatter with a hashtag
and a prayer
because we ride for our men
to the way we ride to the feminist march
with empty passenger seats
because when a Black woman loses her life fighting for
anyone else
she will be considered collateral damage to the cause,
but when a Black woman is beaten, trafficked, or murdered
only other Black women care enough to say her name,
but still

Being a Black woman is lit...in translation,
        it is hell.
Meaning we are constantly burning,
but enduring the flame is our most requested magic trick.
We are to blame when we are not fireproof.
To be Black and woman is to be gas lit so often
the world will accuse you of arson
before they identify your body.

Toyin was a 19-year-old Black woman
at the frontlines of the war against police brutality
while joining the social media movement
against sexual violence,
a movement accompanied by constant Black male
skepticism and silence.
But Toyin still found the strength to share her story.
Days later, Toyin's body was found.
Another Black baby was taken
> *because protection was too much to ask for.*
> *benefit of the doubt was too much to ask for.*

When a Black man falls victim to police brutality,
a Black woman would never ask was he did to ignite such
heat on himself.
We will not ask if his pants were sagging.
We will not ask what they were doing on that side of town.
Those are questions of an oppressor.
Oppressing is a privilege Black women do not attain,
yet when Black women are raped
everyone will ask
> *What was she wearing?*
> *What was she doing there in the first place?*
> *Didn't her parents teach her the dangers*
> *of stepping out of a Black woman's place?*
> So tell me,
who protects Black women when the race war is over?
Who protects Black women when feminism conquers all?

To be Black and woman is to have your skin and gender
constantly throwing up rival gang signs.
Black women are not guaranteed
protection from either set when the smoke clears.
Black women are the only gang where the initiation jumping
never ends.
This tough love is to prepare us for a lifetime of taking blows
from everyone,
so when you see us with the strength to fight back it will look
like *reasonable suspicion...*
Adding queer, trans, or disabled to our fight will feel like a
confession.

Asking for help is like asking to be put on trial.
When a Black woman is silent on these issues
it is because silence feels like the only right that's ever
protected us.
Black women
are always found guilty
until proven worthy of someone who gives a damn,
so you have to give a damn.
Black women do not just matter,
      we are *everything*
and being a Black woman is lit,
in translation:
if you do not help us put out this fire,
we will burn
      everything.

BRIANNA RENAE

I Stalked My Brother's Instagram Today

He is so grown up now.
I remember taking this picture
       – I always take the best pictures of him, but
he posts the worst one every time.
I wish he would show off his smile more often.
       It is so beautiful.
I wish he would show the world how happy he can be
and when I say happy
       I mean *harmless*
and when I say I am stalking his Instagram
I mean am making sure that if he falls victim
to police brutality
       his posts are pure enough to declare him a martyr.
If my brother fits the wrong cop's description
       and this Instagram page is all we have left,
I wonder which pictures they will put on the news.

Will they be innocent enough to start a protest?

Or will the media overflow with
       "we need the whole story" posts?
I wonder if his athletic skills will work to his advantage
or if his build will give justification for
       "fear of life."

I fear that when strangers look at his page they will only see
       his tattoos and Jordans.
I wish they could see the young romantic who would kiss
       Raven-Symoné through the TV.
I wish they could see the superhero
that covered his room in baby powder
       for dramatic impact when he stomped.

I wish they could see the Black excellence
of the young scholar that graduated with honors.

I simply wish the world could see the pure
Black Boy Joy that is my brother.

But I am afraid they will see
       Emmett Till
       Tamir Rice
       Trayvon Martin
       Micheal Brown
another boy whose Black life
will be tossed like a political football,

so when I tell my brother to smile more
I am telling him to give the world a reason
to believe he was worth saving.

This Ain't No Suicide Poem

This ain't the story of the girl who writes one last poem
so everyone can go on YouTube to *really understand.*
This ain't no 13 Reasons Why bullshit.
In Black households
if you got a roof over your head,
clothes on your back,
and food in your stomach,
you ain't got nothin' to cry about.

So like I said,
this ain't no suicide poem.

To be honest,
I don't know what to call this.
This poem is like an incredible itch
that only a pistol can relieve.
Relax,
I swear my finger has never touched the trigger,
but nothing else seems to hit the spot

—I know what you're thinking.
This sounds like a *suicide poem,*

but really I'm just always tired
so I think about sleeping a lot
which turns into thinking about death a lot,
but not in the *sad* way,
in the way that the poor dream of becoming millionaires,
how we fantasize about how all our problems would go away
if we didn't have to worry,
but we know *that's not going to happen.*
        Not to us.
See I love myself

and I love my family,

so *this can't be no suicide poem*, right?
It's only that
going outside has become walking on a minefield
and love does not seem like enough to prepare me
for what's going to blow up next
so I tiptoe around,
sort of like how we tiptoe around this subject.
They say *truth* is the only safe ground to stand upon,
but truth is
standing is
lonely
and I only feel safe in my bed
with the lights off.
Netflix asks me if I'm still watching.
I'm not sure if I ever was
and because the lights are off
I don't see when depression sneaks in bed with me,
wraps her arms around me, casually
asks me why I can never take her outside
and to her I always reply

BECAUSE THIS AIN'T NO SUICIDE POEM.

Depression will give you something to cry about,
she just won't tell you what it is
so you can't talk about it.

You just keep scratching
and *scratching*
until you scrape up enough flesh to justify your pain,
all while your family tells you to be ashamed.
They tell you your ancestors would want you to fight.
They tell you that you were born
so their dreams can stay alive,
but I hate the idea that my ancestors died
running for freedom with bloody feet
just for us to settle into contentment
with basic human needs.
Food, water, and a place to sleep

will never be enough to save the 300 million and counting
suffering from this deadly disease,

but like I said,
this ain't no suicide poem.

III.

Potty Mouth

Now usually I am the soft spoken
Black girl token-
I mean poet,
but after the eighth poem begging for equality,
I was like...
FUCK THAT
I'm going to use these next two minutes to finally snap!
Fuck yo *"All Lives Matter."*
If that were true, you'd be out here protesting beside us.
Fuck ICE for reasons I don't have time to get into,
but I know the hottest corner in hell
is reserved to melt *all of you.*
Fuck that white man that trespassed in **my hood.**
That will always be my daddy's barbershop
and your dreadlocks look like shit!
Matter of fact,
fuck *any non-black girl* that feels entitled to box braids!
I hope your stylist overcharges and they fall out in a week,
BITCH.
Fuck society,
for teaching me that my femininity must cost me my *voice*
and my Blackness my *rage*
because let's be real,
if Black women were granted the rage we rightfully deserve
we could burn down this whole planet
before these two minutes were over!
But instead,
I turn my tongue into an uzi
with sharpshooter mentality
ready to spray any bitch that tries me!

Yet you are the one armed with *bullets*
and all I seem to have is *prayer.*

So yes, sometimes that pisses me the fuck off!
Don't judge me.
Don't guilt me.
Do not make me choose which box you put me into:
peaceful like Martin,
or a *threat* like Malcom
because we both know they end up
in the *same type of casket.*
We both know I will be sealed silent eventually
so I'll be damned if I spend my life hiding my agony,
I'll be damned if my people are
depressed,
crying,
dying,
and you want me to grant you the luxury of my modesty?

FUCK YO RESPECTABILITY POLITICS
We are *HURTING,*

and if the only power I have is to make you *"uncomfortable"*
with my choice of words...
then
GODDAMN
SHIT
BITCH
MOTHERFUCKER
I'll be great at my job!
Because there's nothing comfortable about burning in silence
so if I **die by flame,**
then you damn sure gone **break a sweat, bitch!**
And I know there are only a few seconds left in this rant
so if anything should be taken away
it's that even the sweetest,
most quietest girls like me,
have the right to be
ONE PISSED OFF MOTHERF—

BRIANNA RENAE

Pull Up... I Want My Fade

To the grown men that let me fall for them
then ghosted me because they're "fighting demons",

> *Pull up, I want my fade.*

Deadass,
you have unlocked the final level
black Air Forces wearin' demon
and I am ready to join the fight...
granted, everyone knows I've never been the best at
confrontation,
but I was even worse at trying to love you
and I had one on one archery lessons from Cupid himself
on how to hunt your stubborn ass down.
Left arm aimed at your heart.
Right arm pulling back your reservations until you could see
where I was coming from. When I shot,
you ran,
as Black boys are taught to do,
but Black girls are taught that the work will be twice as hard
and our reward half the size.
I guess I was just trying to be great
and I guess I am trying to find a fancy way to say
I wasted my time.
But on the bright side,
my right arm is now strong as fuck
so when we are face to face,
fist to fist,
I promise you,
I will not miss.

> So pull up, *I want my fade*

Like right now.

There's no "what's wrong babe?
I'm sure we can figure it out."
Nah, fam. That time has passed.
I am here to fuck you up! OKAY?
Isn't this what you want?
Wasn't my tenderness too scary for you?
You like that tough love, huh?
Acrylics all in yo face yellin'
"YOU AIN'T SHIT."
Does this toxicity bring you back to life?
Does it heal yo wounds better than my kisses do?
Bet.

Drop your location.
      I'll pull up my damn self.

And when I get there
I don't want to hear about how you would never
"harm a woman"
because where was that energy
when you carved your initials   .
into my soul just for decoration,
when you loosened up my walls
just to kick them down with your Timberland boots on,
when you looked at me with sad puppy dog eyes
as if my heart wasn't in your mouth like a chew toy
and asked me why I don't like playing games with you?
You know, I think I really might hate you
for turning me into a bitch,
all bark with no bite.
I think I might hate you
for turning my love into the punchline
of the joke we've become.
And I think I might hate myself
because to this day
instead of seeing you as the demon you've become,

I still see a boy hiding behind a façade.

I see a love that would break free if only I got my aim right.
I see a soul that's never felt the nurture of a Black woman

(well, except your mother).
I think that I might hate you
for making me wish I could replace her.
So then I'd have the right to yell your name
when the street lights come on
and I'd ask you

What the hell are you still doing outside?
Don't you know how dangerous it is?
Don't you know how many people wanna see you hurt?
Don't you know you are worth more
than these streets could ever offer you?
Don't you know we all have baggage,
but we are still responsible for who we hurt
when the waste turns toxic?
Don't you know you don't have to carry it all alone?
Don't you know
         you will always have a home in me?
But I will whoop yo ass if you keep walking in and out
of my front door...

But you—
you are a grown man
and I—
was *foolish*
because waiting for you to let me love you
was like waiting for the day
that I—
could ever hurt you.

When A Black Girl Says She Loves Beyoncé

When a Black girl says she loves Beyoncé,
the world often tells her to do so quietly.

They will remind her that Beyoncé
is not a God.
They will tell her there are so many more beautiful things
to love.

What the world often fails to realize
is that a Black girl's love for Beyoncé
is not for the beauty,
not for the superiority,
sometimes it's not even for the music.

Black girl's love Beyoncé for the representation
of all the things we were told we could not become.

Black and woman.

To be Black and woman is to constantly be reminded
there are so many *more beautiful things to love.*

But I refuse to let my love for Beyoncé be small.
I choose to scream my love to the gods,
to my ancestors,
to anyone both willing and unwilling to listen.

And here's why—

Beyoncé turned white girl flower crown wearing Coachella
into Black national anthem singing,
stomp the yard steppin'

"WHO THE FUCK DO YOU THINK I IS?" yellin'
Beychella.
She had me,
a Black woman in Portland, Oregon,
swag surfin' in my living room,
nourishing me with the Homecoming my soul craved.

Beyoncé creates pro Black visual masterpieces.
Black is King gave me the first representation
of African wealth at 23-years old,
allowing me to explore the mysteries of my ancestry
while feeling proud as ever to be a Brown Skin Girl.
Lemonade taught me that pain is generational
and healing is hard,
but nothing real can be threatened.

Beyoncé showed the world pictures of her firstborn daughter,
as any excited mother would do,
and the world was somehow *disappointed*
as if they expected her daughter to be thin-nosed,
blue-eyed
with *good hair*

and instead of hiding from the public
Beyoncé drops a video of her wearing 36in box braids,
dancing in Formation with her daughter,
screaming
"I like my baby hairs with baby hairs and afros!"

Like, are you serious?

Then takes that same Black woman anthem,
performs it at the NFL halftime show
with dancers whose 4C hair kisses the sky
just like mine
in all black leotards paying tribute to Malcom X

because apparently it is possible to be a leader
and *sexy*
and a *mother*
and a *feminist*

72

and *Black*
and **mad**.

Beyoncé defies everything America says
successful Black women should be,

and it's not just Beyoncé that holds this power.

It is also Misses Awkward Black Girl turned cultural curator,
while rooting for everybody Black
Issa Rae,

Miss Youngest Executive Producer
turning her Little dreams into big realities
Marsai Martin,

Miss Hot Girl with three Grammys and knees of steel
writing number one hits between college lectures,
Megan Thee Stallion

Misses Best Selling Author, Becoming the First Lady
with the accolades and the drip,
Michelle Obama.

This is for Black girls changing the game
—period—

and for the creators like *them*
that look exactly like *us*,
that paved the way to make room for celebrations like *this*,
that make young Black girls like *me*
realize this poem should be about myself, too,

Miss Her Way with Words author,
Grand Slam Champ on her first attempt,
healing herself and others with depths of her words,
Brianna Renae.

Can't you see?
Our love is not about infatuation
or screaming *"I Ain't Sorry"*

to dudes who didn't see our worth.

Our love is to say
finally,
this is what it looks like to celebrate
ALL forms of Black women.

So when a Black girl says she loves Beyoncé,
DO NOT MAKE HER FEEL SMALL,
just be thankful
she's inviting you to the party.

Block the Good Dude, Sis

When a good guy comes knocking on your front door
you will think it's April Fools,
an episode of Punk'd,
the result of a lost bet

because good guys don't come around here like that.

When you realize that he is real
you will still sense underlying disbelief

so you do the background check,
ask ya friends about him,
ask ya friend's friends,
stalk his Instagram,
search the county records,
do any and everything to ensure that he's legit

cause you ain't gone get caught slippin again.

But the good guy will check out.
He lets you put your guard down.
He not only loves you,
he teaches you new ways to love yourself.

He is obsessed with your smile—
he says it's captivated him since y'all met.

He says you are beautiful
in a way that shows no possession,
just appreciation.

You think there is no way this guy could hurt you,

he's just too good.

He knows that his goodness is not a reason to rush
so he tells you he wants to wait,
so instead of giving him your body,
you give him your heart

because that, you believe he has earned.

The good dude tells you
"You deserve the world."
And your heart rejoices
for all the bad ones
that made you feel like too much,

but not him.
He says
"Know your worth Queen, then triple it."
So that's exactly what you do,
but that price is not one he can pay to you...

So the good guy does the unthinkable
and it breaks you.

You will try to deny it.
No.
It can't be him.
He can not leave me.
He's not like those other guys.

And you are right,
he is not,
which is exactly why he must let you go,

and this is exactly why you must
block the good dude, sis.
Because good is not enough reason to stay with someone.

When we are so used to being treated like shit
we will hold on so tight to the good ones
even if they aren't *the* ones
because they are better than the bad ones.

But good dudes can hurt you, too.
And they can be bad at taking care of themselves
and you have to believe them when they say
they are not capable of taking care of you.

Be thankful for the gems
good dudes drop on your doorstep
and willing to wave goodbye
when it's their time to leave
because good does not guarantee they will stay
and love is not enough
to heal a sad boy whole again.

Take care of yourself first, sis,
text that man 'thank you' for knowing your worth
and leaving you alone if he can't pay the price.

Block his number,
and pray that God and therapy
bring him nothing,
but the best.

BRIANNA RENAE

Skin Hunger

In psychology there is a term called 'skin hunger'.
It describes our need to be touched
and the consequences that may occur with the lack thereof.

Day 1

The idea of you never touching me again
has yet to cross my mind,
but my stomach rumbles every time I think of you.
I know I am sad,
but have no idea how hungry I will soon become.

Day 8

I notice the physical changes.
Without you I am so much smaller.
My body is feeding solely on the memories.
As I shrink,
I remember less and less what you taste like,
how satisfying your name feels in my mouth.
I panic.

Day 9

I relapse
through tasting you all over again.
I realize that without you
I was starving.
Did you always satisfy my soul like this?
What is it about things that are bad for you
that makes you want to indulge so recklessly?
But as I go for the next bite
you remind me my emptiness

is no longer your responsibility.

Day 13

I frantically try to substitute your touch
with my own.
Tracing my own skin,
intertwining my own fingers,
searching for your residue in the crevices of my thighs,
but my touch does not bring back the meat
already fallen off my bones.
It does not stop my stomach from screaming.

Day 17

I have to eat something.
Malnutrition caused this desperation.
Searching on Bumble and Tinder
for a fast food type of touch.
Don't judge,
Taco Bell could make a vegan water at the mouth
if you starve them for long enough.
Some call this a hoe phase,
but I call it
survival.

Day 33

If you are what you eat
then I am
disgusting,
but at least my belly is full.
Binging on high fructose fantasies
—nothing that I want—
they fill me,
which is exactly what I need...
but now this gluttony doesn't sit well.
I regurgitate it all after every meal,
knowing this half ass love will not digest,
but feels so good being swallowed.

Day 36

I can't go on like this.
It is time for a detox.
Cleanse out the toxins
and the toxic temporary satisfaction.
I meal prep
because waiting until near death to seek nourishment
is always a bad idea.
I plan ways for my needs to be fulfilled
—platonic and consensual—
consume the feel of healthy relationships
when the skin hunger kicks back in.

Day 47

I realize recovery is possible,
and damn it tastes so good.
I wink in the mirror.
and smack my own ass
as a reminder that I am four course fine as hell
and no matter how hungry I get
I am still whole.
I am always enough.

BRIANNA RENAE

One Day

One day
I am going to be *happy*.
One day the dean will read my name followed by *cum laude*
as I walk across the stage with multiple degrees to my name.

One day
I will not have to fill out job applications,
corporations will be calling my phone off the hook
begging me to represent their brand.

One day
I will write a poem about Michelle Obama,
she will repost it on her Instagram and I will be known
as the "Michelle Obama Poem Girl"
—I will be so famous Beyoncé will use snippets of my work
as the intro to her next hit single.

One day
I will meet a boy who will see my value
without having to show him a price tag.
He will remember small details about me,
like how I love blueberries muffins on Saturday mornings
and he will make them for me every week.
He will know how much I love the little things
and give me all of them.

One day
I will get married.

One day
I will make love
and I will call them my child,
I will make sure they love their brown skin and coiled hair
way before the world tells them it isn't enough.
I will cut their sandwiches
in the shape of their favorite animals.
I will write *"mama loves you"*

on their favorite colored sticky note every day.

One day
my child will hurt, cry, bleed,
and nothing will stop the pain, but mama's kisses.

One day
I will be needed.

One day
I will be happy.
But I do not know when that day will be.

So today,
when the words of my textbook are spinning
fast as my doubts of ever graduating,
I won't stop reading.

Today,
I filled out an application
—they called to ask about the gaps in my resume.
I couldn't tell them that I've been mentally and physically ill
and the idea of being at a job full time
has me trembling as we speak
so instead I say
"I took time to take care of myself,
but now I am ready."
This may not be enough,
but one day it will be

So today,
I wrote a poem
and it was nothing like how I pictured it in my head.
It was nothing Michelle would ever repost,
but instead of deleting it I saved it
and I keep editing it periodically
because I know one day I will love it.

Today,
it is Valentine's Day
and I am alone.
Not just single,
but alone alone.
I am sad,

but peaceful.
I spent today alone
because I refuse to spend tomorrow half-loved.

Today,
I made myself blueberry muffins
—I called this the blueprint of how to love me properly.

Today,
I do not have children,
but I stop to compliment little Black girls' hair in public.
I volunteer with kids every week,
I make sure they never forget the power
in their little soft voices,
I remind them that they can be anything they want to be.
As they do the same for me.

And today,
that feels like enough.

Today,
there might not be a person that walks this earth
that would die without me,
but I need me.
That is enough.
Today I am trying.
That is enough.

Yesterday,
I didn't wanna be here
so today,
I am learning to love that I still am
and tomorrow,
I swear,
I will be happy.

Happy Birthday

A letter from 19 year old Bri:

So tomorrow I turn 20. I want to say "time flies" but it really didn't. These years have gone by very slowly. But when I stop to think about the fact that I've been alive for 20 years, it sounds really long. When I was 14 I was full of life, but then my Crohn's Disease came and a part of me left that I wasn't sure could come back. At 16 I didn't want to be myself anymore. I thought the world was going to hurt me
so I hurt myself before anyone else could.
I searched for love in shallow waters, avoided mirrors and church at all costs. I did not realize the damage this would do, nor did I care. When I turned 18 I didn't want to be alive anymore. All the pain from heartbreak, losing my relationship with God, my family, losing my 'virginity', and most importantly myself, finally caught up to me. Voices came into my head, causing me to spin until I'd fall unconscious, wanting to die without the blood on my own fingers. I hadn't said a prayer in years, but if I did, it would be for God to show mercy and end my misery for me. I became numb to life. So much love surrounded me,
yet I was blind and alone in my head.
I didn't do it though.
On my 19th birthday I wanted to be different. I couldn't be a victim to my own faults anymore. It was hard to even accept the fact that I was the only person stopping my happiness. It hurt, but it was the best decision I've ever made. I went to therapy. I opened up for once. I started writing again. I started performing again. I became more focused on school. I accepted the fact that I was broken, but was open to the idea that I could be healed. "You always fuck shit up" turned into "your best is the most anyone could ask of you, keep pushing." I quit my jobs and took care of myself. I let people back into my life and learned how to live again. I started messaging old friends on Snapchat. Driving to see family

more. Laughing more. Loving more. Accepting more. Still crying, but growing from it more. Learning to forgive, but no longer accepting toxicity in my life anymore. I told myself I am the shit and that anything I want is within my reach.

I just have to keep stretching. Always forward.

I learned to love myself and the life I have. Hiding from the mirror turned into staring at myself naked, and smiling. Dancing. Blowing kisses. Saying I love you, and I love you back. Laughing extra hard at my own jokes. Going to coffee shops alone. People watching in my car. Meditating. Bonding. Growing. Always forward... And tomorrow I turn 20. And I thank God for allowing me to say that. I want to thank my 16 year old self for making me learn hard lessons at a young age, and praise 18 year old me for never pulling the plug. It would be a shame for me not to live my life to its full potential, even if that's what scares me most. I have so much love to give in a world so cold. I realize that my heart is so pure. My care is so tender. My ambitions could change the world. I now realize how much of a shame that would be if all of that went to the grave

before I even got a chance to blossom...

I am sitting on this airplane to Miami. They do not have wifi so that is why I am writing this. I am sitting here reflecting on my life and I can finally say I am so proud of myself. Lord knows I have been to hell and back several times, but I deserve my wings. I can't wait to see what 21, 22, 23, even 60 year old Brianna has to say. I just pray that it is always forward. Of course I am far from where I want to be, and I have a LOT of improvements to make. But I can honestly say I am better than the person I was last year and that means the world to me.

I'm so anxious to see the things that I will accomplish.

Even if I do not live long enough to reach my peak, I'll be more happy to die living, than to never have lived at all. So my advice to future Brianna would be not to forget the lessons you've been teaching yourself your entire life. Stay you and stay humble. Live more Bri, you deserve it.

Happy Birthday,
I love you,
Breezy '17'

Meet Brianna Renae

Brianna Renae is a spoken word artist from Portland, Oregon. She started writing poetry as a coping mechanism to heal herself. She transformed into an author when she discovered that Her Way with Words had the capability to heal others as well. Brianna's poetry will take you on an emotional ride as she explores themes such as activism, vulnerability, and raw Black Girl Magic.

Brianna founded The People's Poets open mic in 2017. She created this platform so that writers of color can feel the power and liberation of telling their story. Brianna Renae was crowned 2018 Grand Slam Champion and represented Portland at the 2020 Women of the World Poetry Slam. She has featured for many great organizations such as Pickathon, WeMakePdx, Literary Arts, and many more. Brianna has something to say, and is thankful for anyone willing to listen.

Instagram : brianna_poetry

Facebook: Brianna Renae Poetry

Youtube: Brianna Renae